TERI FR

MW00953161

THE
FUNNY THING
ABOUT
THE TRUTH

outskirts
press

The Funny Thing about the Truth
All Rights Reserved.
Copyright © 2021 Teri Franklin
v2.0 r1.2

This is a work of fiction. The events and characters described herein are imaginary and are not intended to refer to specific places or living persons. The opinions expressed in this manuscript are solely the opinions of the author and do not represent the opinions or thoughts of the publisher. The author has represented and warranted full ownership and/or legal right to publish all the materials in this book.

This book may not be reproduced, transmitted, or stored in whole or in part by any means, including graphic, electronic, or mechanical without the express written consent of the publisher except in the case of brief quotations embodied in critical articles and reviews.

Outskirts Press, Inc.
http://www.outskirtspress.com

ISBN: 978-1-9772-4563-2

Cover Photo © 2021 www.gettyimages.com. All rights reserved - used with permission.

Outskirts Press and the "OP" logo are trademarks belonging to Outskirts Press, Inc.

PRINTED IN THE UNITED STATES OF AMERICA

DEDICATION

To my mom, Willie Bell Kyles; (Forever My Bell), my sister, Vicki "VIC" Kyles; you are forever in my heart, my father, Albert Kyles Sr. (Without you, there would be no me) my kids, Taniyah, Vikkia, Chad, Justin, Kevin Jr., my grandkids, 1 thru 6 Meliyah, Nasir, Nyell, Phoenyx, Noah and Jason, and of course, those that are fans.

Contents

ACKNOWLEDGEMENTS

I would like to thank God for blessing me with such an amazing writing gift and giving me such creativity and courage to follow my dreams.

To my family, thank you for the love and support.

To my mother Willie B. Kyles (May she rest peacefully in paradise) who have always loved me unconditionally and told me I could do anything that I put my mind to. She was my number one fan from day one. I wrote my very first poem to her, and even though it was the traditional **Roses are Red Violets are Blue** poem, she loved and cherished it. The display on her dresser made it even more special. So, thank you mama for always believing in your baby girl.

To my husband Kevin T. Franklin Sr. for being a good support system, and always being there when I need you most. All that you do for me is greatly appreciated and it will never be forgotten. I love you to the moon and when I reach the stars, I'm bringing you with me!

To my children, from the oldest to the youngest, Taniyah, Vikkia, Chad and Justin. I love you guys with every beat of my heart. If my heart should every stop beating, just know that each one of ya'll had a piece of it, and that's on real love.

To my siblings, Sandra; Michele; Albert; Timothy; Kimberly; Doressa and Fritzi (Let's stay together) I love ya'll. I'm glad I'm not an only child.

To my listen to this, let me read this to you right quick crew, Taniyah; Vikkia; Chad; Denisha; Nicoshi; and Anna. Ya'll have great ears!

To my God son Shane Nelms who is my troubleshooter for everything! He is going places in life!

To Troy Henderson AKA Mizter Man who is also a poet and my long-time friend. I had the opportunity to collaborate with him and put our creative thoughts together and express our poetic feelings, all while having fun creating a poem which we called "DIVORCE". You are an amazing writer, and I cannot wait for us to write another poem together.

To my son Chad Sinclair Bryant, a brilliant self-taught artist who continues to strive for nothing more than perfection in all his pieces of art. I am so thankful for you letting me showcase such amazing art throughout my book. Continue following your dreams, they do come true!

To my club sisters of Tulip L. Jones Women's Club, East Palo Alto, California. Dorothy Busby (RIP), Barbara Perkins (RIP), Lucile Strong, Gloria Mason, Stacey Kennon, Sandra Pickrom, Michele Kyles, Starli Hampton, Nicoshi Marzette, Anna Hodges, Portia McLemore, Kimberly Kyles-Wyche, Lisa Campbell, Sherri Bundy, Detra Sledge, Stephanie Robertson, Adeshina Burley, and Sonja Rogers. We are so proud to be a part of the same organization that Madam CJ Walker was a part of, The National Association of Colored Women. "Deeds Not Words."

To Cherrese Wilson-Brown, Barabara Pasana, Joshua Simmons, Chad Bryant and Justin Franklin, thank you for letting me utilize such beautiful and amazing pictures. Pictures can express many words and your expressions says a lot.

To my dawg, my ace, my ride or die, my sister-cousin, my get mad at each other today and talk to you tomorrow BFC Anna M. Hodges, thanks for telling me all I do is write poems all day while at work. LOL that motivated me more. So, thank you MEG!

To Starli R. Hampton my shining star! Thank you for shining such a bright light when I asked you for title suggestions. There was no hesitation, you said let me pray on it and I will get back to you in a couple of days. You kept your word. You called me with excitement and said it came to you…and now… "The Funny Thing About the Truth is here. Much Appreciated!

INTRODUCTION

I found my courage to write this book, when I started looking in my closet and seen all the journals that I had written poetry in. I realized that someone might be interested in hearing what I have to say. So, with that being said… I started thumbing through the pages and laughing at some of the things that I had written. I said to myself girl this is too funny, and it is true. It is real-life situations that people go through on a regular basis. I am sure there is somebody out there thinking it, but do not want to or know how to say it. So, I figured expressing for them can be relieving for many people whether it is factual or fictional, that is how I think some-times. Most of it is relatable, I write on experiences whether it is mine, somebody else's or even yours. The Funny thing about the truth is…It's true!

The funny thing about the truth is…
No one likes to hear it
No one likes to face it
No one likes to believe it
And no one likes to live in it

Section 01: Black Lives Matters

A Closed Mouth Don't Get Fed

When you stand in the background and never say a word.
You get the feeling that your voice will never be heard.
Don't be silenced learn to speak your piece.
Using your voice is powerful.
And you have the right to freedom of speech.
Don't stand in the background without speaking out loud.
Or your voice will forever be drowned out by the crowd.

Black Man, Crack Man

You see that man.
That's a black man.
That's a crack man.
Doing the best, he can.
Because he let the dealer.
Deal him a bad hand.
And he literally can't stand on his own two feet.
Homeless sleeping on a cardboard box on the street.
He's full of filth.
And nothing to eat.
It's a situation that he's in because of bad choices.
Having solo conversations.
And answering to the voices.
It's sad and a shame.
That so many brothers end up like that,
Because drugs were calling their name.

Have Mercy

Black as soot,
Hot as hell,
California is burning,
Holy grail.
Cars burned up and homes destroyed.
Lives and a lifetime of belongings lost.
Sentimental things of value irreplaceable at no cost.
Unimaginable temperatures of heat.
While firefighters are tirelessly on their feet.
God have mercy on us and let the ones we've lost rest in peace.

"My eyes are dry but my tear ducts are full"

Blessed

Every day is a blessed day
Live it like it's your last day
There are no promises or guarantee for another, week, month, or year
Get on your knees and pray that God will hear
Don't worry about judgement only he can do that
People will try to block your blessings and that's a fact
Ask for forgiveness and forget about the past
Just thank God that today wasn't your last.

Hood

He's hooded
But he's not a thug or a thief
Not looking for trouble or beef
He's not going to rob
He's not going to steal
He's not going to kill
He's just a black man wearing what he feels
Hoods pump fear to those with a racist and ignorant mentality
And the sense of fear on which they are feeding
Everybody knows that looks can be deceiving
And it's the mothers of black men who end up grieving
A hood is just a hood
And it doesn't mean that every black man that wears one
Is up to no good!

Mad Black Woman

I'm a mad black woman and I know it
You walk all over me and I'm gone show it
Put a stone in front of me and I'm gone throw it
All that's been done to us it's time to expose it
My anger is real and it's over loaded
I'm a mad black woman and sometimes I have no filter
If you push my buttons, I'm off kilter
I'm a mad black woman who have to prove who I am
I'm Black and I'm Proud and I'll say it again
I'm a mad black woman because they don't want me to be me
I'm a phenomenal woman, the apple didn't fall far from the tree
I'm a mad black woman because they don't treat us right
And all of our lives we had to fight
I'm a mad black woman because they keep killing my people
And every day there's another sequel
And they just won't treat us equal
I have a right to be a mad black woman
Because racism won't stop
And equality isn't coming.

"Humiliation is not the end of your world, perseverance

is the beginning of your new world of happiness"

Mirror Mirror

Mirror Mirror in front of me
Black and beautiful is what I see
Voluptuous thighs and my beautiful breast
While I admire the skin I'm in
My birthday best
Embracing me for what I see and who I am
A reflection of a confident sistah
who don't need confirmation from a man
When I look in the mirror
I like what I'm looking at
As my long-braided hair lay on the small of my back
I remember that dark chocolate is like an aphrodisiac
And the beauty about me is
Embracing that I am Black

Nickname Rona

Who is Rona and how did it get here?
It shut us down for a whole year
Rona came through like a thief in the night
No warning signs just taking millions of lives
Taking folks out without warning or a short notice
While nothing but negativity came from the POTUS
Pointing the finger and placing blame
This is definitely not a racial thang
Rona came in and took lives now the world is forever changed
Jobs and wages were loss and bank accounts were drained
People became homeless, they started robbing and stealing
There were even people with suicidal feelings
So many people caught the virus and had to die alone
They were admitted to the hospital but never made it home
This virus is real
I can't express how other people feel
I hope the feeling is mutual, and I'm not alone
I wish I could say poof
And it would all be gone!

The Simmons Era

There's a time and a place.
Fighting for equal race.
I'm a black man.
Respect my space.

"I don't care what ya'll think
I just want you to think
Open the box and think outside of it
And stop living in it"

Strong Black Sistahs

Stop being a sistah hater

I know that you can be anything that you want to be,
but don't let that be who you are

Sistahs need to be uplifted, not let down by each other

Sistahs don't need to be body shamed because of their size,
they should all be confident and wear it with pride

Sistahs shouldn't fight each other, they should learn to fight together for
our equal rights

Sistahs need to learn how to reach out to each other, instead of
disrespecting one another

Sistahs need to be mature enough to know that they bring drama too,
and it's not always the other person

Sistahs need to learn how to be happy for one another,
their time will come

Sistahs that have life figured out, shouldn't degrade those that don't

Sistahs need to have each other's back, instead of talking
behind their backs

Sistahs can't love each other, if they don't love themselves

Sistahs need to empower each other, instead of making each other
feel powerless

Sistahs need to shine their light on each other if they are full of sunshine

As sistahs we all have our own faults and none of us are perfect

But loving your black sistah is well worth it

Sistahs might not always get along, but at the end of the day
we are black sistah strong!

True That

I'm trying to live in Black America but there's no equality
I'm crying out for help; can you hear me?
No justice No peace
These cop killers are irritating me
The political system is full of injustice and racial discriminatory
No punishment just a slap on the wrist and that's the end of the story
There's too much racial bias and they continue to try us
We've been fighting for years
What our ancestors' fault for with blood sweat and tears
We want to be treated equal, we don't want a systemic sequel
We've come to know that white is always right
And brown and black will never win the fight
Number forty-five has turned this world into a debacle
And it will never be the same
We want justice for Breanna Taylor…SAY HER NAME!
There were so many others treated the same
The list goes on with so many names
This system has truly failed us
And it is hard to be black in America
They dare us to say it loud
Because we are black, and we are proud
All people should have equal justice and rights
It should not matter if you're black or white
But as blacks in America
We had to fight all of our life.

When Black Don't Match

We put each other down
We disrespect one another
We don't trust each other
We don't respect each other
We fight each other
We degrade our men
We don't trust our women
We don't motivate each other
We don't educate each other
We try to eradicate one another
Let's make Black magical again
So that everyone that is black can win

Section 02: Love

Attitude

I never bring sand to the beach I strut alone.
I stroll and I peep to see what's in my reach.
I used to be worried about what people think.
So, I had to get my mind and my attitude in sync.
"Stop questioning my thinking until you've read my thoughts"

"No repetitive apology is worth excepting,

When you are conscious of what you are apologizing for"

Broken Love

Love is a four-letter word
That can be divided into two
It's either something you're feeling, or something you do
And when it's real love you'll know it's true
But love can be blind, don't let it blind you.

Granted

Have you ever been taken for granted?

The L in love was slanted, and all the other letters followed

Because the real meaning of love was swallowed
by someone that want to be loved

But don't know how to give love in return

Take your heart and tie it up so no one else will love you better

Because you are confident and of purity

But they will not let you go because of their own insecurity

You offered all that you have, and you gave all that you could

If the denominator isn't common, the love ain't no good

Your love is EVOL and stale…in other words a backwards ass
LOVE that initially fail

Because not one person should be taken for granted,
because only real love will prevail

He Ain't What You Think

To love a handsome man means to recognize his worth beyond his physical appearance.

A man's arrogance and inferiority complex can transform him into a monster.

Beauty isn't always everything.

Everything else will fall into place if you look for his softer side, spirituality, and compatibility.

How Deep

His love is deeper still and he keep giving me something I can feel
I keep getting butterflies in my stomach so it's got to be real
He gives me chills, frills, and thrills
Kisses me from my head all the way down to the heels
Of my feet, licks back up my thighs then to the middle to eat
He gives me his chocolate with cream on top
Hard like I'm pole dancing just to keep things hot
Like fire and he wants to make it rain
Awe shit I think I came and he went
A little lower bent me over and stroked a little slower
Because his love is deeper still and I love how it feel
He has a stroke that's smooth and makes me groan
Nicknamed his penis captain foot long
Make a sistah never wanna leave home

I Am

I am all I am
I am all I have
I am all I can be
I am me

It Seems to Hang On

The funny thing about love
Sometimes it works and sometimes it hurt
We long to be in love because that is what our heart feel
But sometimes love can be a gut punch as if it is not real
How could love be gone when it was just here?
Love was so inseparable
And now you love each other to tears
love can be so strong but with a few words it is all gone
I thought that love was unconditional, but something went wrong
Neither one of us are new to this game
Love is like a rollercoaster
It goes up and down
And just when you think you are about to lose the love of your life
true love always seems to hang on.

Keep it Moving

I lost my motivation, my concentration, and my determination
I'm reluctant to believe that we can achieve what it used to be
So, I'm feeling free
Bird style
Like ready to fly
Now that I'm ghost in the wind you're ready to try
But time keeps on ticking even when the love won't last
And all those feelings become a thing of the past
But they won't be forgotten in the future
Situations and scenarios keep playing in my mind like old songs grooving
and I need somebody to put the batteries in my back
So, I can keep it moving.

Lies

Lies don't die they multiply
A habitual liar can lie effortlessly,
Painlessly and unforgivingly

"Telling a little white lie and getting away with it is one thing,

but telling a lie in black and white there's no denying"

Love Hurts

Sometimes love hurts more than it feels good
Don't be the next victim or misunderstood
Although it may hurt get out if you could
Domestic violence cases are going up more than they should
Phone a friend or find a hiding place
He's choking your throat but next is your face
If he can't love you then you need to leave him
Stop conditioning your mind to believe you deserve to be abused
You should never be taken for granted or sexually misused
Emotions and fears run high, while your self-esteem is low
Getting your ass whipped, you thought to be a lifestyle
because that's all you know
Every breathe was constantly taken away, while feeling alone,
embarrassed, and guilt continued to grow
It wasn't your fault, you were intimidated and manipulated
You were giving him your love because it was something you yearned for
You wanted a love that was true, but it was something that he couldn't give you
Never joy, only pain
Ask yourself who's to blame
You said you left him maybe once or twice
Then took a chance on coming back like rolling dice
Why would you come back to a nightmare like on Elm Street?
Do you want to be pushing up daisies from under six feet?
Get out girl while you can
He is more like a coward and less of a man.

"Always judge a toxic person
By their toxicology report
Otherwise, they will poison you with toxicity."

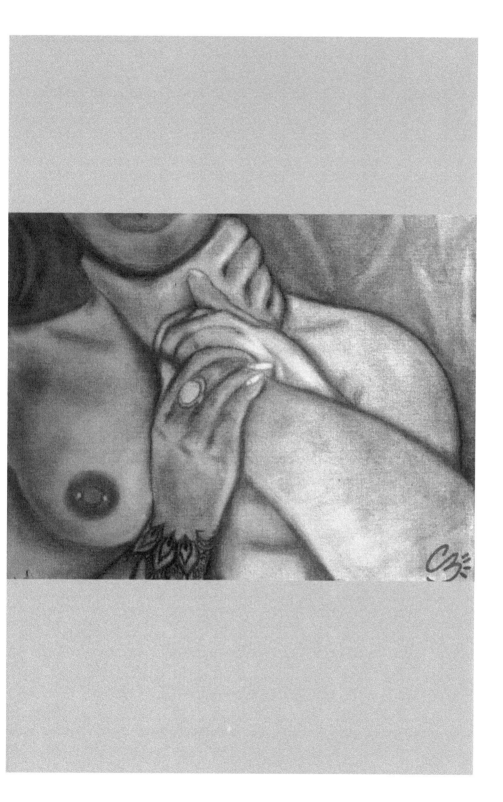

Love or Not

If you are not ready for love
Don't open your heart valve
If you are not ready to commit
Don't make a commitment
If you're not ready to trust and honor
Don't say I do
If you need and want love pursue it
If the love is real
Give it your all
If it's infatuation
Don't break hearts or manipulate minds
If you are in love
Love shouldn't be questionable
So…love or not

On the Other Side of Love

Love is pain
And this creeping is driving me insane
I let you come and go as you please breaking my heart every time you leave
Knowing that you have a wife at home with needs
Why are you here with me?
I know that I can't replace her or have you to myself
It's a one-way street and I'm in another woman's lane
And I know that you will never love me the same
But that's on me because I let you play your game
I've been a fool for so long and I can't take it back
You are never leaving home and that's a fact
I guess I got used to the material things
That was part of your plan
And me being on the other side of love I just wanted a man
Now I realize that you will always love her
And you ain't going nowhere
I must admit ya'll are quite the pair
So the next time you knock on my door
I can honestly say to myself
I'm not going to be on the other side of love anymore.

Sage Em'

You steal my joy all the time
You kill my noise when I speak my mind
It's like being a prisoner of love
Love ain't what it should be, and it definitely ain't what it was
I go into shutdown mode
I can't get my point across, it's like a dead-end road
My happiness is not your happiness
The heart is tore and material shit don't move me no more
You're like a joy-thief seeker
It gets cold and dark; you remind me of the grim-reaper
I can't find that happy medium
Because you won't meet me halfway
It's a constant debate with you everyday
You're self-centered in an egotistical way
It's like sitting in the middle of war, but I am at peace
I can't let you keep stealing my joy
So, I'll sage you, until your negativity is released.

Secrets

I want to tell it all
But I gotta keep in mind that my reputation is also on the line
I know a closed mouth don't get fed
But some things are better left unsaid
But I know and you know what's true
I ain't gone spill the tea yet
I'm just gone let it brew.

The Truth

The funny thing about the truth is…
That most people live in their lies rather than their truth
The bigger the lie the harder it is to tell the truth
And as the lie get bigger there just ain't no use
Lies come and they go
I've watched some of the most influential peoples nose grow
Every day is a challenge to find the solution that reflect your truth
Sometimes it can make you laugh and sometimes it will make you cry
Either way your brain is working hard to remember the truth and the lie
Every liar tells the opposite of what they really feel in their heart
If you don't believe nothing else, believe that part!

Under the Moon Light

Meet me tonight at the beach with the jet-black sand
The yellow full moon will be bright as we hold hands
The waves will be crashing upon the shore
Our bodies close together wanting more
The ocean breeze and the smell of fresh air
Your eyes are as lusty as you continue to stare
I'm wondering if you can take me there
As I whisper softly and seductively in your ear
I want you to sweat profusely as the sound disappear
Cum now, hold me tight and close your eyes
It's a beautiful feeling as we lay until the sunrise!

Vows

Before God you vowed
Before God I vowed
Things were said like to love and to cherish until death do us part
We both watch the infidelity start
Vows and hearts were broken
Side pieces became tokens
When the shit unfolded no one was laughing or joking
Things were denied
Patience was tried
Eyes cried
And alibis were frequent when coming home late from work
Whole routines changed and that shit hurt
Secret phone calls and plenty of text was no longer a secret
Because we weren't having sex
And all I could think of is who's next?

Section 03: Women

Battle of The Bitches

I'm a bitch
You're a bitch
She's a bitch
And sometimes he's a bitch
Why battle a bitch?
A bitch put up a battle
A bitch put up a fight
A bitch gone battle you
Whether she's wrong or right
Punk bitch
Trick bitch
Disrespectful bitch
A bitch ain't shit
Don't get caught up in bitch shit
If you know you ain't a bitch.
"You can always tell when a hungry bitch is messy
Because you can feed her some bullshit
And she's gonna share the recipe."

Comfort Zone

Get out of your comfort zone
It seems as though it's keeping you from moving on
It seems as though you're having a tough time following your dreams
The first step is not as hard as it seems
Your life can only change if you stay committed to what you want,
And stop being comfortable where you're at.

Birds

Birds of the same feathers typically flock together.
But your wings are so unique.
I've watched you spread your wings and fly to your own heights.
I've watched you peck at your goals and when they were met.
You flew on to your next flower of happiness.
A hummingbird is unique.
They are special and represent joy and happiness.
Always fly high and continue to HUM to your own tune.
For a bird is a bird, but a hummingbird is you

Decrying Me

Can you see, feel, hear or read the words that are coming out of my mouth?
What gives you the authority to tell me what I should talk about?
It seems as though you didn't agree with what I said
Why should it matter to you? Did I get in your head?
People are so quick to judge a book by its cover without reading the content
I said what I said, and you read what I meant
It's too bad that you were so bent out of shape
I'm talking about what I want to, so let that marinate
What's on my mind shouldn't be concerning you or up for debate
I hope you get the message, or should I reiterate?
Wait...did you read something that angered you?
Because you're not the one I'm referring to
If you think I'm male bashing, then let me bash
You must be one of the ones who wrote a check their ass couldn't cash
I know that men aren't the only ones who do wrong
However, they are the ones with the same dance and song
So, if I talk about men in every poem that I write
It's my freedom of speech
So don't be uptight
You BEN-done!

Fly

If I could fly away with the wind beneath my wings
I would forget about what was and explore the possibilities of new things
I would fly off into another space and time
Elevate my thoughts and stimulate my mind
I want the feeling of being stress free
I want to see what else is in store for me
I want to fly into new heights
No worries at bedtime just peaceful nights
I wanna fly so high where the air is crisp and clean
I wanna forget about what misery loves company mean
I want to fly like a bird without broken wings
I want the hummingbird effect, I want to sing
I just wanna fly away and spread my wings

Giving Body

Our breast
Our hips
Our thighs
We all have that melanin drip
But we are all a different size
Afros, afro puffs and braided hair
We are embracing our heritage like we just don't care
We walk the walk
We talk the talk
We are highly intelligent
And we are cut from the same cloth
We are embracing our body
And to others we may be perceived as naughty
It's all in the vision of what you see and how you feel
These are some unapologetic sistahs keeping it real!

Overdue

It's coming to me
It's all starting to come together
It's been a long time coming and my motivation is so much better
So much to talk about and so much to say
Shout out to those who heard my voice and knew I was on my way
It's almost like a reprieve, somebody was blocking my blessings
But I accepted and received
This insane writing gift that was given to me
I guess I better use it or lose it
Talk about what I know
And let other people hear how I flow
It might be some truth in it
Or just my imagination
However, I deliver it, it's my recollection
Some of it will make you laugh
And some of it will make you cry
Some will hit home, just know you are not alone
Either you are going to love it, or you are going to hate it
Instead of taking it personal, I think that you can relate to it
I just hope that you will share it, and if the shoe fits wear it
People love drama, and what is true
I hope you read the whole book
These poems are for you.
"My mind is occupied right now; I'm wrapped up in my thought"

I Love Words

I write because I love words
I write because I want my voice to be heard
Writing gets complicated sometimes
But just learn to read between the lines

"How can you be yourself if you always worry about
What the next person thinks of you"

Life, Love & Encouragement

What do I owe you that you think I haven't already given you?
I gave you life, love, and encouragement
Three essential tools
It's up to you to use them
Your life is up to you how you live it
Your love is how you give and receive it
Your encouragement is seeing and believing
Your success is you chasing your dreams and making them come true
Living your best life is up to you
Everything you think that I do not do for you I already done
When I gave birth four times my struggle begun
And being an adult was no longer fun
I couldn't hide or run
I was a go getter, made do with what I had until I could do better
I wasn't asking nobody for a doggone dime
I got out and worked for mine
Tell me again what I haven't done for you
Or when I wasn't there
When your chips start falling
Let me know who else really cared because mama will always be there
If I could turn back the hands if time
I 'd choose the same four to be mine
So, don't ever tell me what I don't do for you
That's a bunch of bull
Consider any IOUs paid in full

My Cup Runs Over

I have waisted years

I have waisted tears

Negative energy around me and I'm trying to conquer my fears of
moving on

Being strong and stop holding on to false hopes and dreams

With no definition, meaning or explanation how I have arrived
in this situation

That is making me sad and blue

And being untrue to myself happiness that I know I'm capable of having

I don't want to be crying

So, I keep laughing

Phat Ass

The Phat Ass ain't mine
The Stock of the day
The Fucking Peach
The Badonkadonk
The Miss Butterworth
The Donkey Booty
The Big Booty Judy
The Apple Bottom
Ain't none of those asses mine
If a Phat ass is what you need in me, you are wasting your time
The phat ass ain't mine

Reinforced

Stop throwing bricks at me
I already laid my foundation
It was just enough to make me a successful woman
So, thank you for thinking I wasn't strong enough
I didn't know my own strength.

Respect Yourself Sistah Without a Doubt

Respect yourself sistah without a doubt
Keep your lady like and your dignity and don't let your ghetto out
hold your head high, walk like a stallion and don't be caught off guard
Because it's a cold cold world, and us sistahs got it hard
So don't be out there acting ignorant and talking loud
Remember your representing the Black and proud
Respect yourself sistah without a doubt
I once heard that the lessons of a fool ends up without
No pride, No confidence, No self-esteem
We just make it harder to live the American dream
They say that talk is cheap, so don't let that be your distraction
For years all the white girls got all the satisfaction
And I'll be damn if I settle for a decimal instead of a fraction
Of the all mighty knowledge that's like a fatal attraction
Respect yourself sistah without a doubt
I was also told that ignorance was to have and to hold
And that the black sistahs was scared to let their knowledge unfold
Truth be told you should let your diva out
And let the jealous have something to talk about
Be respectful
Act dignified
Be true to yourself and swallow your pride
Let the respectful sistah out you have nothing to hide

Restless

In the wake of the night
I lay there restless and relentless
Staring at the ceiling as if I'm in a strange place
Not watching the clock, no time limits
But a fight to win my own race
My eyes and my mind wide open and I know why
I'm a goal getter and I can't get there if I don't try
There's no sheep for me to count
And no bottles of beer on the wall
I just gotta leap out on faith and not worry about the fall
My wheels are spinning so fast
I'm afraid my mental notes won't last
Because my thoughts are many
Noises throughout the room, I hear
Sounds like…you can do it in my ear
I know that success has no sleep in it
And I have nothing to fear
So, I stay woke because my success is near

Routine

Lock and load for years
The same routine can drive you to tears
Change something
Switch up
Let up
Ease up
Grow up
Stand up for a dream and make it come true
Step out of your comfort zone and be all of you
Magnify your thoughts
Stop justifying your failures
Count your blessings
Look at your negatives as life's lessons

Simplicity

It's the little things that make me happy
I like holding hands while singing my favorite love song
I like little trinkets in cute little boxes that I can keep for so long
I like laughing until it hurts
I like jeans and tee shirts
I like dancing until I'm weak at the knees
I like playing in the park and hiding behind trees
I like long drives with the sunroof open so I can feel the breeze
I like the simple things
So, simplicity works best for me

Skid Marks

Who walked all over me today because I allowed them too?
Was it you?
Was it her?
Was it him?
Or was it all of them?
I hope you walked the distance that you were trying to achieve
Because I see them bruises on your knees.

Unsupported

Have you ever had dreams, goals and plans?

And someone talked you right out of them?

Made you think that dreams don't come true

And your goals were impossible too

Your plans were just okay, and they tried to talk you into doing it their way

What do they know about dreams coming true, when they don't believe in dreams at all?

What do they know about reaching a goal, when they continue to help you fall?

What do they know about implementing plans?

When you have all the tools but they snatch them right out of your hands

But your eagerness and inspiration to move forward is strong

But the jealousy keeps holding on

Weighing you down with negativity

Helping to keep your dreams in captivity

Don't ever let someone else catch your dream before you make it come true

Especially when you have plans and goals that you have already thought thru.

Strong

I stay strong because I have to be
In fear that if I crack it's going to cause insanity
I stay strong because it's the black woman in me
In fear that I might not be strong enough to keep my strength
I stay strong because if I fall it might not be as easy to get back up
In fear that the fall may be harder than it seems
I stay strong because my strength is measured by my faith
In fear that if I lose that mustard seed, my faith will be gone
I stay strong because I cannot shed any tears
In fear that someone will hear me crying
I stay strong because I'm hurting inside
In fear that no one will feel my pain
I stay strong because strong is all I can be, and all I am
In fear that the strong in me you will never understand
So I stay strong...

Today's Anatomy

Tummy tucks and Brazilian butt lifts
What happened to being all natural with Gods gifts?
Lips filled with collagen
Cheeks plumped with Botox
Eyelash extensions straight from the box
Colored contacts in all the different shades
European weaves and micro braids
Piercings and tattoos to cover up a bruise
What happened to our brown skin that used to me so smooth?
Facial skin pulled back really taut
Nose reconstructed without giving thought
Stilettos and wedges 4 to 6 inches
While heels and toes are over extended
No more mani and pedi's that's simple and plain
Acrylic and Gel are the hottest thang
No more tanning by sun rays
Everybody wants what's man made
So don't be mad at me
It's just Today's Anatomy

What Makes It Good to You?

When he makes you feel good from your head to your toes

And you want to shout and scream

That is the man of your dream, and he will crown you because
you are his queen

You don't have to ask for nothing, he will give you everything

You can leave all your worries behind because true love is hard to find

When he makes love to you, he will make you feel so go inside

You will never have insecurities that you have to hide

It is your world

Live in it

Give in

Love in it

It is your fantasy

It is your glory

I am just helping you believe in your love story

Love do not come by chance, it's an attraction

Everybody gets a chance to love, but do not get the same reaction

Lucky for you, you get it all and not just a fraction

If you do not have to be in a relationship that comes
with the sharing prerequisite

He is the one, that is your man, he's the shit!

All About Me

I keep forgetting all about me
I keep forgetting to love me
I keep forgetting to hug me
I keep forgetting to trust me
I keep forgetting to touch me
I keep forgetting to see me
I keep forgetting to be me
Because when it is all about you
There is no me.

"Depressed shopping temporarily eases your mind while draining your pockets, until you come back to reality and be like…why in the hell did I buy all this shit?

Where's my receipts?

Section 04: Relationships

Blind

Seek and you will find
We all know that love is blind
Don't keep looking for confirmation for something you already know is true
When your lover keeps doing the same shit to you
It's just confirmation that ya'll are really through
Don't start begging and pleading for your lover to stay
Let what don't wanna be there go, and what do come what may
People are always on that thin line
You know the one between love and hate?
Open your eyes, so you can see
Stop the foolery and set yourself free.

Dear Mama

Dear mama you were our queen, and we were jewels in your crown
Your smile was so radiant
I can't recall a time when there was a frown
You meant everything to me
You were the absolute best
You grew tired and I understand that you were ready to rest
You were a phenomenal woman to me
You birth me
You nourished me
And always encouraged me
You loved me before I knew what love is
You are the only woman I know that had so much love to give
You did the best you could, and you did it on your own
You ran the show with no father in our home
You taught us how to be ladies, and to keep it lady like
You taught us self-respect and dignity, and we turned out alright
You told us to treat people the way we wanted to be treated
But, also not to settle for less if we are not treated equal
You taught us as siblings to love each other from the heart
Not knowing you were prepping us for the day you had to depart
Now I understand what your love and long talks were about
We would have lots of friends, but family is first no doubt
You opened your heart and doors to many
Although you did not have much to give, to others it was plenty
You were cherished and loved so much
I thank God for the time you had with us
As we stood around your bed after you took your last breath
It was hard to let go, but peace filled the room as your wings started to grow
Your spirit took flight, and you flew away
I miss you so much, I still cry everyday
You were a peace maker and truly kind

Some way or somehow, I wish I could turn back the hands of time
But time moves forward, and you are a beautiful angel of mine
There is so much more that I have to say, that I should have send then
I could keep writing but this poem would never end
There is no one like a mother, a protector, or who is also your friend
So, I will just wait until I get to heaven when we reconnect again.

Divorce

I remember that day in early May
The birds singing
Our families rejoicing
I felt our love was strong
Solid...
What a great foundation we built it on
As the year flew by
Our love pushed aside
Where did we go wrong
Was it me
Singing that same old song
The tension in the air
Do we have to go there
All that we have accumulated
Split down the middle or should it be investigated
Divorce is such a harsh way to go
Is it true that you don't love me no mo
Can I fix it
Is this the last straw
I'll fight to the end
Don't leave me
Don't take it all

Wait you musta forgot who you were dealing with, becuz a sistah don't play that shit

You can take the Porsche and the Range, but the Bentley is gone remain in the garage that we won't be sharing any more,

This has turned into war and hell, because you fell to be the husband that I thought you would be, but instead you cheated on me

So now you gone pay the cost

And trust me it ain't no luv loss

You destroyed this marriage walking around with your new baby in a carriage, so now you gone suffer the consequences

You fucked up and got double expenses

So give me mines

I want what's coming to me

And don't tell judge Mathis

You only can pay monthly

You play, you pay

If nothing else you gone learn today

So take these divorce papers and leave me alone, when I get home from work today I want you gone.

You cold

You bold and the Bentley is old

Yeah, I slipped got caught with my zipper unzipped

But you ain't no saint

Walking around like yo shhhhhh don't stank

No cooking

No cleaning

All you were doing was begging

If it wasn't for me you wouldn't have that weave

When was the last time you brushed yo teeth

Now don't get me wrong

Our love use to be strong

But when a brotha got that new position

You thought you were Louise Jefferson

I tried to make you happy

You had it made in a shade

A maid

A cook

A driver

You even had someone to turn pages in your books

Oh and the Judge

Don't trip...

We golf together

So trust and believe

If I pay you, it will be a small fee

If you had any sense

You would stay like Magic's Cookie

Or you can take your chances and hope like Jordan's Juanita

Either way....

This won't be a big pay day

You got me twisted

I see you been drinking

I'll be gone bout time you get home

But I'll be back later on with Judge Mathis on the phone

Okay this is it...
Now you just talking bullshit
You know ain't none of this shit true
You just exaggerating like you always do
And you think Mathis is on your side
He keep begging me for a ride
And don't think I won't pick up a hitchhiker
And I ain't worried about his wife
Cause I don't even like her
And no I don't wish I was like Juanita or Cookie
I'm a professional not a rookie
You ain't the first husband that I took to the bank
So after I take all your money
Tell me what you thank
Oh...
And don't think I ain't gone have nothing left
Cause you was a gold digger yourself
Tell me, is this real
When all you do is beg, borrow, and steal
And then you gone talk about brushing teeth
I got one question, where's the beef?
Best believe you can have it your way
Cuz I'm through with your ass starting today
What? I don't here no more laughter
So after today, less close this chapter

(By: Me & Mizterman)

Flame

There's still a flame and it's lit
He love's my swag he said I'm the shit
And if I don't come correct, he tells me this ain't it
And I'm all natural without big hips
I don't need fillers because I have nice lips
And he knows I'm not a gold digger because I stack my own chips
I'm not a groupie but I know some VIPS
I keep it interesting, so it's never hit or miss
Don't try to take notes so you can walk in my shoes
Cause they ain't gone fit
But if your coin is right, you can purchase my survival kit
So your flame won't burn out
It will always be lit

He's Married

Are you comfortable loving a married man?
Who already have a wife?
How could that be real love
Is that how you live your life?
He belongs to someone else, and you are fully aware
I guess when you are lonely and by yourself, you don't seem to care
If loving him is wrong, why don't you do right?
You can't be seen in public places
But you are a bed warmer by night
You have a beautiful soul and mind
But the way you are going about loving someone
You will never have a man to yourself in this lifetime
"Don't try to read another woman like an open book
Because ya'll had a disagreement
Some books aren't worth reading
Not even the rough draft"

I Don't Know You

There's a stranger in my house
I was misunderstood when I thought everything was all good
Got me sitting up here like I wish a nigga would
You ain't the same person I met
You've done all kinds of shit that's hard to digest
Some of it forgivable and the others hard to forget
And I still haven't left
There's a stranger in my house
And it's filled with gloom
Don't shit happen but sleep in our room
I'm upstairs and you're downstairs like I'm not near
Texting another bitch saying you wish she was here
Talking about what you cooked and how you were chilling
But if I did that shit you would be in your feelings
There's a stranger in my house with no regrets
When I'm looking for love it's just soft and wet
There's a stranger in my house
And I'm waiting for him to come clean, but he ain't came clean yet
All the shit you've done, I don't think I will ever forget
Give me an apology, I deserve that much respect.

I'm Here

I might not be your best friend, but I'm a good friend
I might not know what to say, but I'm a good listener
I might not always know how to help you, but I can get you help
I might not know how to handle your feelings, but I'll handle them with care
I might not know your triggers, but I'll try not to pull it
I might not know what makes you happy, but I can help make you smile

Keep It

What I hear, I keep
And what I sew, is what I reap
So, I strive to be the best me
Times are harder than they used to be
Ain't no more us and we
most people are living by… you for you and me for me
Things ain't always been that way
I remember back in the day
when people loved, cared and respected one another
Households was strong with a father and a mother
Heads were bowed and on bending knees
Yes sir, yes ma'am , thank you and please
Kids were kids…they laughed…they played…and they learned
Nowadays our elders get no respect
because this new generation thinks it should be earned
and you can't teach or tell them nothing
that's a synopsis of how the tables have turned
What I hear, I keep
And knowledge runs deep
Education is essential
And reading is fundamental
Wisdom is given by the wise
Learning should never be compromised
Ignored or despised
What I hear, I keep
And I slept on a lot of opportunities that I should have seen
Mama always told me
nothing comes to sleeper but a dream
so now my knowledge is inestimable
I've learned a lot in my lifetime
I'm always pressing play and never rewind
There's no off button in this entrepreneurs mind

The harder you work
The sooner you'll see your work start to manifest
Optimism and knowledge will be your key to success
But ain't nobody gone give it to you
You gotta do for self
What I've heard, I kept
I've asked
I believe
And I accept
What I hear, I keep
What I hear, I keep
What I hear, I keep
And if you're familiar with the "Secret" that's what I keep!

Let a Player Play

Some relationships are like playing a game
There's a bunch of players
Everybody gets a turn
Everybody loses a turn
When you are tired of the game and you want to quit
Walk away and the game will be over
when you stop playing

Love Me to Tears

You tell me you love me
But you love me to tears
My emotions are so mixed, I'm spinning like Buzz light year
You always say I'm overacting when I call you out on that
Tell me exactly how I should react
I will not be second to none
When I started off as number one
You can't have your cake and eat it too
That's some male chauvinistic shit you're going thru
You let someone else's pussy power tear us apart
And I will not be the one with a broken heart
It might be time for us to part like the red sea
You're into the players life and that isn't man enough me
So you go on and live your life like you're single
I think it's time for me to get out and mingle
I shouldn't be in tears or spinning
If love ain't true, we both need a new beginning.

One Nighter

I'm dick happy and you want me to call you pappy

But I'm not looking for a relationship or a sugar daddy

I just want you to touch up the nappy

Hairy chin snowed up like Santa, I guess you are someone's pappy

I just want to get mine and send you home after I unwind

Don't drop your jaw men do it all the time

The same scenario but a different line

Remember when dudes only wanted to hit it and quit it?

But chicks wasn't really wit it, they were just young and dumb
and full of cum

He would tell you what you wanted to hear and then
he had to make a run

Payback is a bitch and men should know

That some women don't let that shit go

Note to self…all dick ain't good dick and the way this world is set up,
you gotta think quick

Don't be amazed by some wood that look like a broom stick

You might lay down with a prince

But you will end up on some frog type of shit

These feelings aren't from the present this shit is past tense.

Pregnancy

Imagine loving someone before they even know what love is
The feeling of movement and a thump, as I touch my baby bump
I smile at you all the time, while baby names are on my mind
How precious and so sweet, the pitter-patter of kicking little feet
A mother's love is something that never ends
Nine months of pregnancy, then a new life begins
Happiness and joy will fill the room
When you make your grand entrance from the womb
Nurturing and caring for you every moment of your life
Motherhood doesn't come with instructions, but you learn what's right
I promise to take good care of you every day and every night
This amazing feeling inside my stomach makes me smile
It's truly a blessing to be caring my child.

Shit

Everybody's going through some shit
Everybody's been through some shit
Everybody talks shit
Everybody thinks they are the shit
And nobody really gives a shit!

"When people make you feel under appreciated
You don't have to always react
Fuck You will be more understood than the reaction"

Sisterhood

Hands of Love
Hands of Peace
Hands of Joy
Hands of Happiness
Hands of Friendship
Hands of Sisterhood
The power of sisterhood and friendship
Will always have a strong connection!
Are you connected?
Is your friendship true?
Every sistah should have a powerful connection that solidifies their friendship
What does all these things mean to you?
Stay connected!

The Bone Collector

You should have been a bone collector because your closet runs deep
So many skeletons it's a wonder you can sleep
You toss and turn in the bed
Visions of the past going thru your head
You can't stop lying and believing yourself,
you can't get rid of them bones because it's too many left
Will you ever be able to clear up your conscious that causes your
relationships to be like a stave
Or are you taking this one to your grave
They say that ghost come back to haunt you
But bones that's not buried deep enough will continue to taunt you
Your love for me is like a curse from a old ritual back in the day
It won't let me leave so I continue to stay,
hoping that one day you'll come clean and wash all your bones away.

The Second Time Around

The thoughts of marriage the second time around

The fear of uncertainty going through my mind

I thought about my previous marriage and how it broke me
and went down hill

As I gaze off wrapped up in my thoughts, I know that this is GODs will

Everything feels so right, how could it go wrong?

Our mental relationship was two years strong

Our minds were in sync as we texted on our phones

I didn't want to mess up a good thing

I didn't want it to be gone

It was an experience that I never felt

And I didn't know that my heart would melt

Now I'm standing here on my wedding day

I love this man in every way

And I can't take what I am feeling back

He proposed to me, it was so surreal that I had a panic attack

I know that he is the right man for me

Our friendship has proven how true love is supposed to be

I know that I am the woman for him, and all the woman that he needs

My mind and soul were empty

Now my heart no longer says vacancy

So, I'm gonna walk down that isle and face my fears

When my eyes welled up, they were happy tears

And when we say "I DO"

We will be thankful for our blessings because our love is true

So, here's to conquering my fears and marrying once again

You are my lover, my husband, you are my best friend.

The Silent Wife

Living a married life in silence
Silently seeking revenge
She moved in silence and never told her friends
She never uttered a word of all the allegations she heard
And as much evidence as there was to the contrary
Her payback was coming by all means necessary
Would it be a crime to lay all the deceitfulness on the line?
How you treated her, and thought that shit was fine
How you broke her heart, and manipulated her mind
Here comes her sweetest revenge
It's game time!

"If time heals all wounds
What time does the healing begin
And how long does it take
The wounds to heal?"

Unraveling

When does a relationship that's hanging on by a thread throw in the towel?
Does anyone know how?
Don't everybody speak out of turn so fast!
Isn't true love supposed to last?
Does the whole towel need to unravel?
Does the whole towel need to turn into shreds?
This conversation is often heard but never said
It's funny how people be acting like their relationship ain't dead
Couples be out there fronting, getting nominated best supporting actor
When the relationship been a non-factor
And that's on unraveling.

"When you've been leaping alone and haven't been caught yet
It is difficult to trust that someone will catch you
trust will be a leap away if you trust that you will be caught."

All artwork is created by Chad Sinclair Bryant aka King Bookem, of Sinclair Art Studios.

Chad was born and raised in the Bay Area where there is Hella Talent.

He is a self-taught artist and have been artistic since a young age. He reclaimed his passion for art a few years ago. He have been doing amazing work ever since he has picked up his pencils, canvas and paint brushes.

www.studiosinclair.org
IG: Kingbookem
FB: kingbookem onset bryant

CPSIA information can be obtained
at www.ICGtesting.com
Printed in the USA
BVHW022058161121
621766BV00014B/302